AROUND THE WORLD IN EVERY VEHICLE

NZ 123

SCENIC FLIGHTS

The little blue
camper van

Quarto is the authority on a wide range of topics.

Quarto educates, entertains and enriches the lives
our readers—enthusiasts and lovers of hands-on l

www.quartoknows.com

Author: Amber Stewart
Illustrator: Duncan Beedie
Consultant: Felicity Fitchard
Editor: Ellie Brough
Designer: Verity Clark

First published in 2018 by QED Publishing, an imprint of The Quarto Group.
The Old Brewery, 6 Blundell Street, London, N7 9BH, United Kingdom.
T (0)20 7700 6700 F (0)20 7700 8066
www.QuartoKnows.com

A catalogue record for this book is
available from the British Library.

ISBN 978 1 78493 872 7

9 8 7 6 5 4 3 2 1

Manufactured in Shenzhen, China
HH052018

MIX
Paper from
responsible sources
FSC® C017606

AROUND THE WORLD IN EVERY VEHICLE

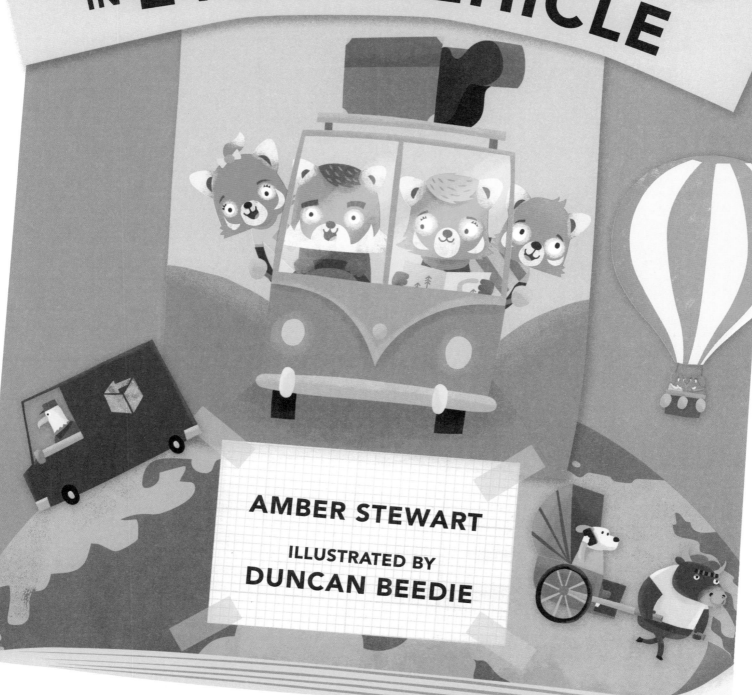

AMBER STEWART

ILLUSTRATED BY
DUNCAN BEEDIE

QED

The Van Go family love their quiet, little corner of the world in Scotland in the United Kingdom.

Every day, Freddie and Daisy cycle up and down their street with friends.

Mum and Dad Van Go fill up their bicycle baskets with food and goods from the local shops, and visit with Grandpa and Grandma.

But there is a **big**, **wide world** out there waiting to be explored.

The little street will still be there for the family when they come home.

They have planned their long summer break, and the Van Go family are heading on a round-the-world trip!

One final check of passports, tickets and travel money and it's time to pack up their little blue camper van . . .

. . . and start their **big** adventure.

London is their first stop! London is **noisy** and **busy**. Tourists snap pictures in Trafalgar Square.

Black taxi cabs drive round and round at Buckingham Palace, looking for fares. They weave between cars and bikes and the big red buses.

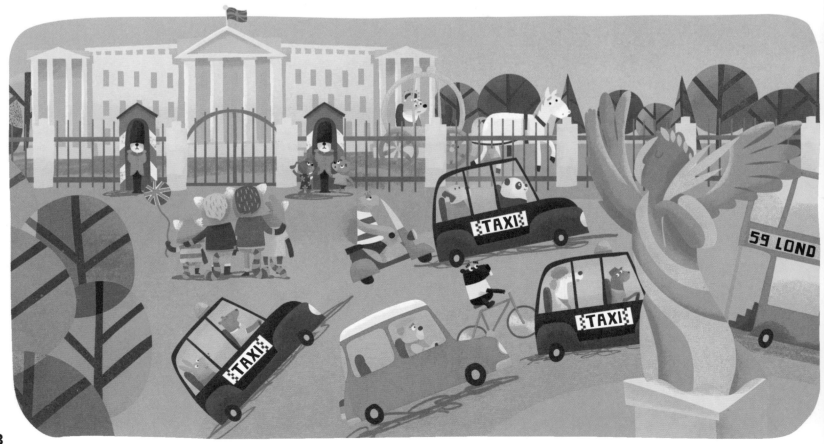

The Van Go family take an open-topped bus tour, sitting high up to see the sights.

"What other kinds of buses can you find around the world?" Freddie asks, opening up his journal.

Yellow School Bus - USA

Passenger Bus - SOUTH AFRICA

Tour Bus - ITALY

Greyhound Bus - USA & CANADA

In the morning, the Van Go family arrive in Folkestone, England. They look at the signs.

~PRIDE OF THE SEA~
CHANNEL SEAWAYS

"Are we going to France by ferry?" asks Daisy.
"We're going under the water, not on the water!" says Freddie.
They are taking the car train through the Channel Tunnel to France.

The car train is quick. Soon they are driving through the French countryside on their way to Paris. They watch the farmers working on the land with tractors, trailers and combine harvesters.

11

The Parisian streets are a whirl of excitement!
Cyclists scoot past them, with baskets full
of shopping. Taxis beep and honk along
the Champs-Elysées.

The Van Go family are going to explore the city by metro.
But Freddie is nervous about going underground.
"Don't worry, Freddie," Mum Van Go says, "many cities have
metro systems. They are a fast and safe way to travel."

All the routes out of Paris are busy, busy, **busy!**
"I think all the Parisians are going on holiday today,"
sighs Mum.

Horns honk, drivers
shout, everyone is hot
and bothered in the
three-lane traffic jam.

Slowly the traffic clears and the little blue van rolls through France and into Germany. They follow the River Danube, stopping along the way in pretty villages.

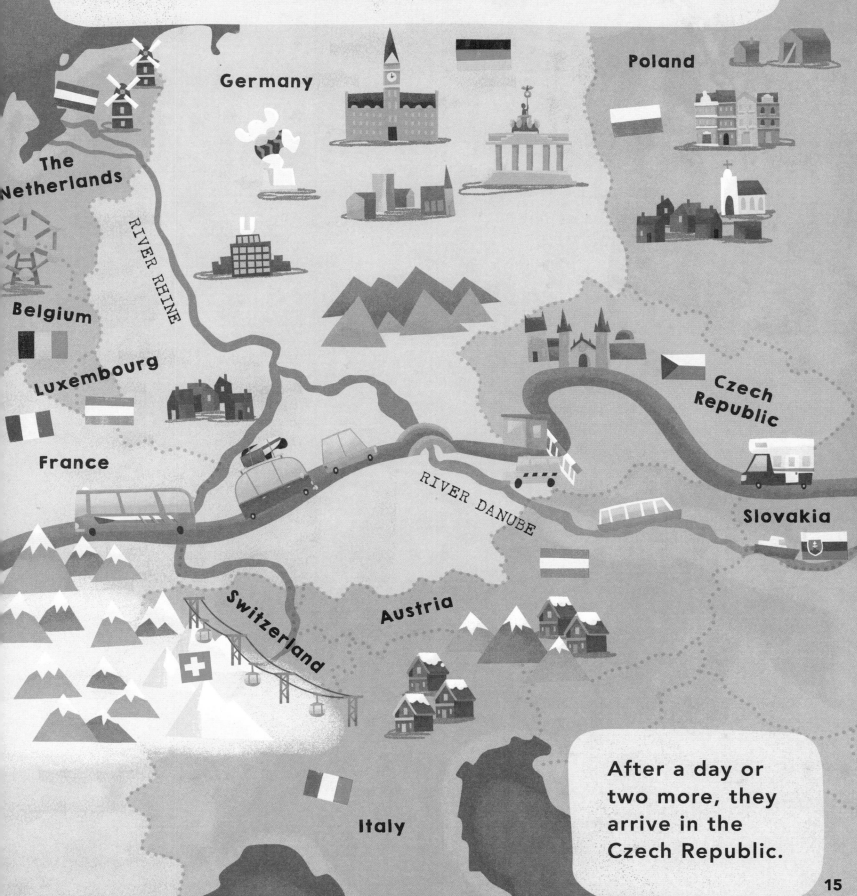

The Netherlands

Belgium

Luxembourg

France

Germany

Poland

Czech Republic

Slovakia

RIVER RHINE

RIVER DANUBE

Switzerland

Austria

Italy

After a day or two more, they arrive in the Czech Republic.

The Van Go family has never seen a city like Prague!

As they walk slowly over Charles Bridge, Daisy and Freddie wave to the people but they don't wave back. "Those are statues, not real people," smiles Mum.

CLASSIC RIVER TOURS   221

A friendly policeman waves instead, directing traffic this way and that. He shows Daisy and Freddie his police car.

"Police cars look different in other cities but they all help to keep people safe," he says.

NYPD - USA

Keisatsu - JAPAN

Polizia - ITALY

Police - AUSTRALIA

The Van Go family now face quite a test – four days driving across four different countries!

SERBIA to BULGARIA 390km

BULGARIA to TURKEY 550km

ISTANBUL 102km

18

CZECH REP
to SLOVAKIA
330km

COLA

SLOVAKIA
to SERBIA
570km

Did the little blue van make it? Of course it did: it's the best van in the world!

Istanbul is bustling after dark!

They explore the city by tram.
Voices echo from the decorated
mosques and the streets are full of
laughter and chatter from the cafés.

TAKSİM TÜNEL

TAKSİM TÜNEL

San Francisco - USA

POWELL & HYDE Sts.

27 SF

Melbourne - AUSTRALIA

KEW DEP.

159

159

Amsterdam - THE NETHERLANDS

S CENTRAL

GVB

Lisbon - PORTUGAL

CARREIRA Nº. 28

"Next trip we can visit other famous cities with trams," says Dad Van Go, as he holds on tight.

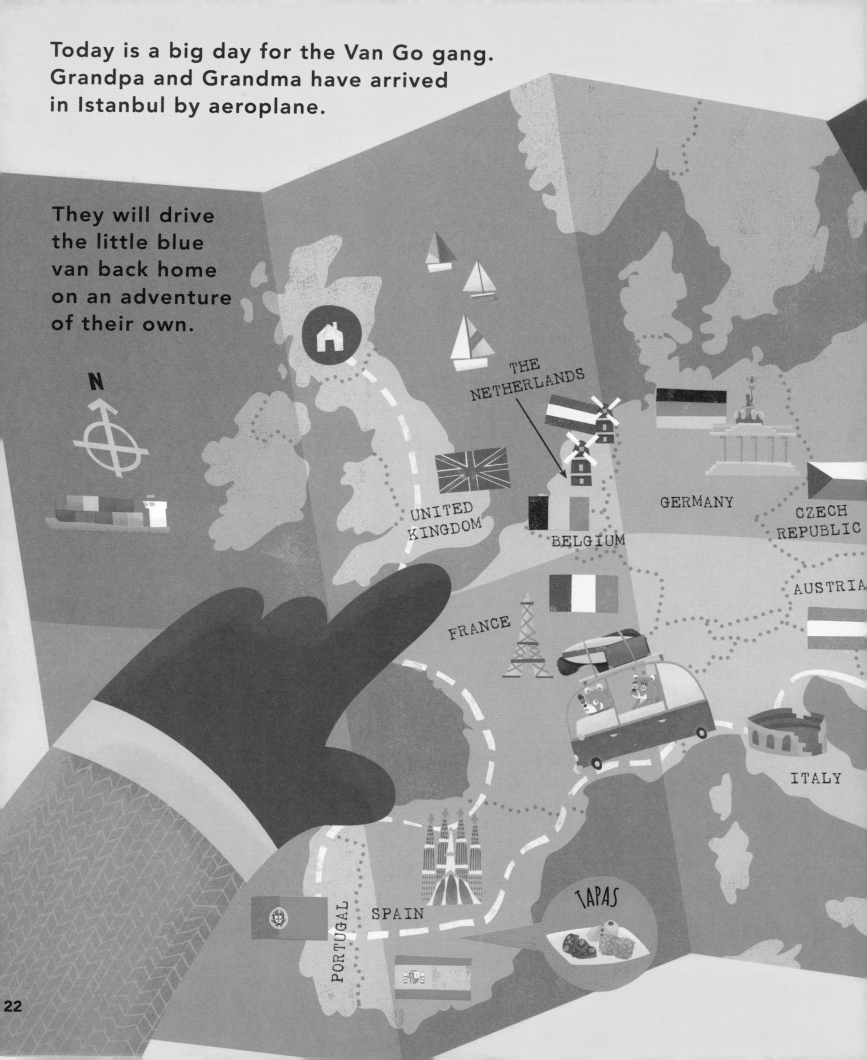

Today is a big day for the Van Go gang. Grandpa and Grandma have arrived in Istanbul by aeroplane.

They will drive the little blue van back home on an adventure of their own.

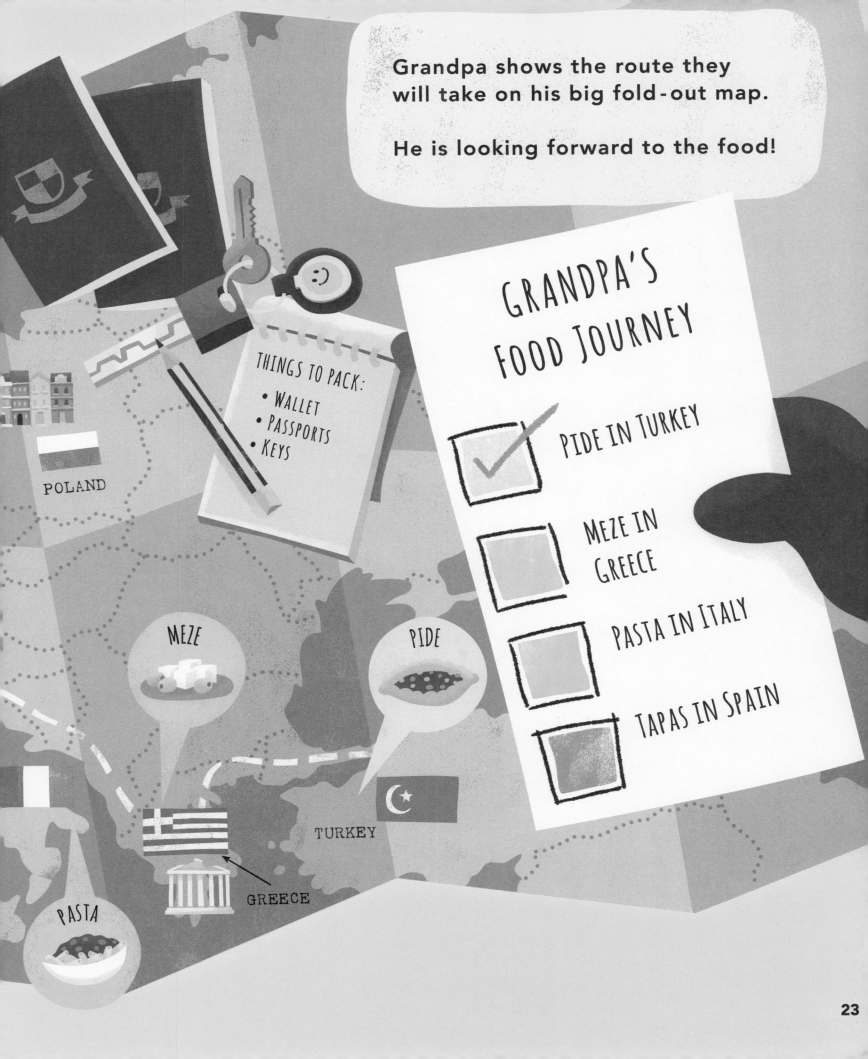

Grandpa shows the route they will take on his big fold-out map.

He is looking forward to the food!

THINGS TO PACK:
- Wallet
- Passports
- Keys

POLAND

MEZE

PIDE

GREECE

TURKEY

PASTA

GRANDPA'S FOOD JOURNEY

☑ PIDE IN TURKEY

☐ MEZE IN GREECE

☐ PASTA IN ITALY

☐ TAPAS IN SPAIN

The Van Go family are sad to wave goodbye to Grandpa and Grandma but eager to get to the airport to continue their travels.

Freddie and Daisy have never travelled by plane before. Excited, they show their passports . . .

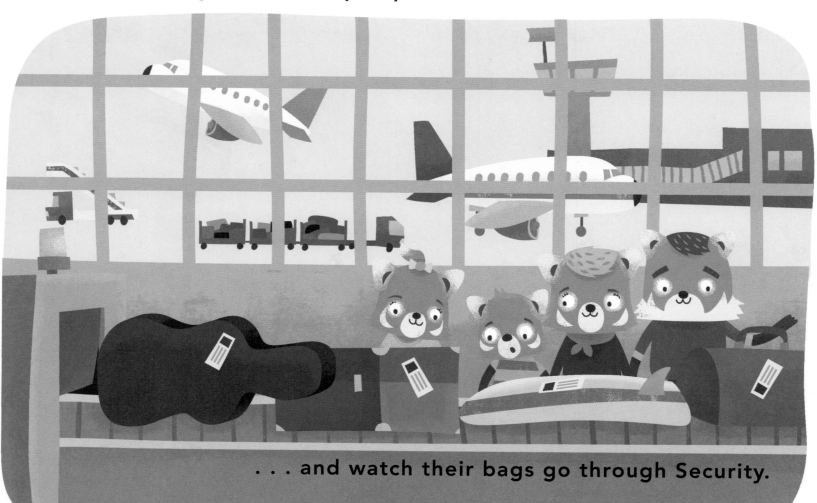

. . . and watch their bags go through Security.

The Van Go family will fly to Mumbai in India, in a huge jumbo jet. At the airport, they see planes of all sizes.

While waiting to take off, Daisy looks up other sorts of planes.

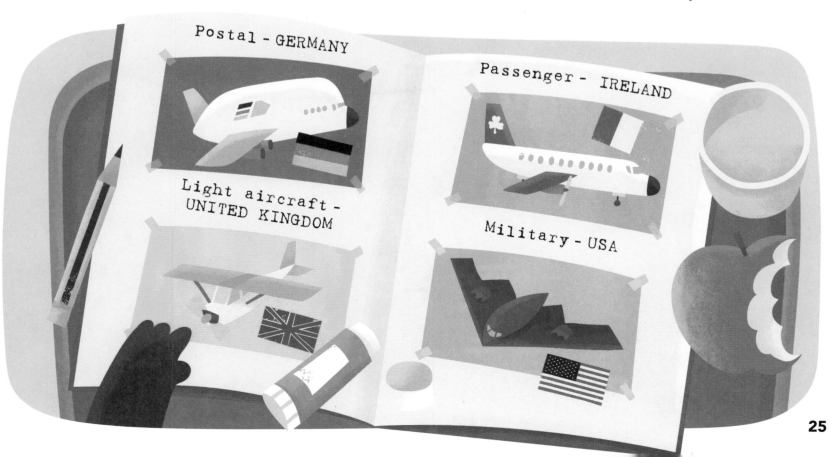

Postal - GERMANY

Passenger - IRELAND

Light aircraft - UNITED KINGDOM

Military - USA

After nearly seven hours in the air, they land smoothly in Mumbai. The Mumbai streets are colourful and noisy. Cars and buses, bicycles piled high, rickshaws and tuk-tuks all travel this way and that.

They have arrived during the famous food truck festival.
"That one reminds me of our little blue van," points Daisy.

The Van Go family love the food cooked and served
from colourful trucks.
"Let's do a food tour one day," laughs Freddie.

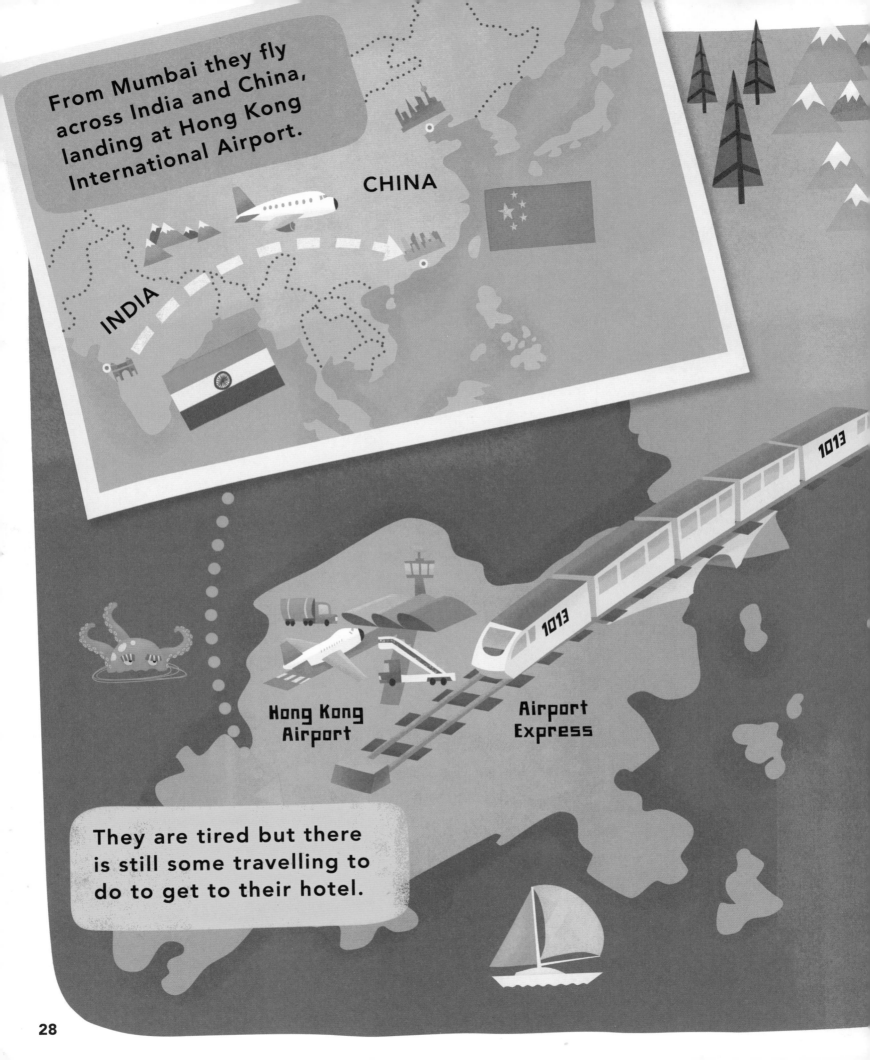

From Mumbai they fly across India and China, landing at Hong Kong International Airport.

CHINA

INDIA

1013

Hong Kong Airport

Airport Express

They are tired but there is still some travelling to do to get to their hotel.

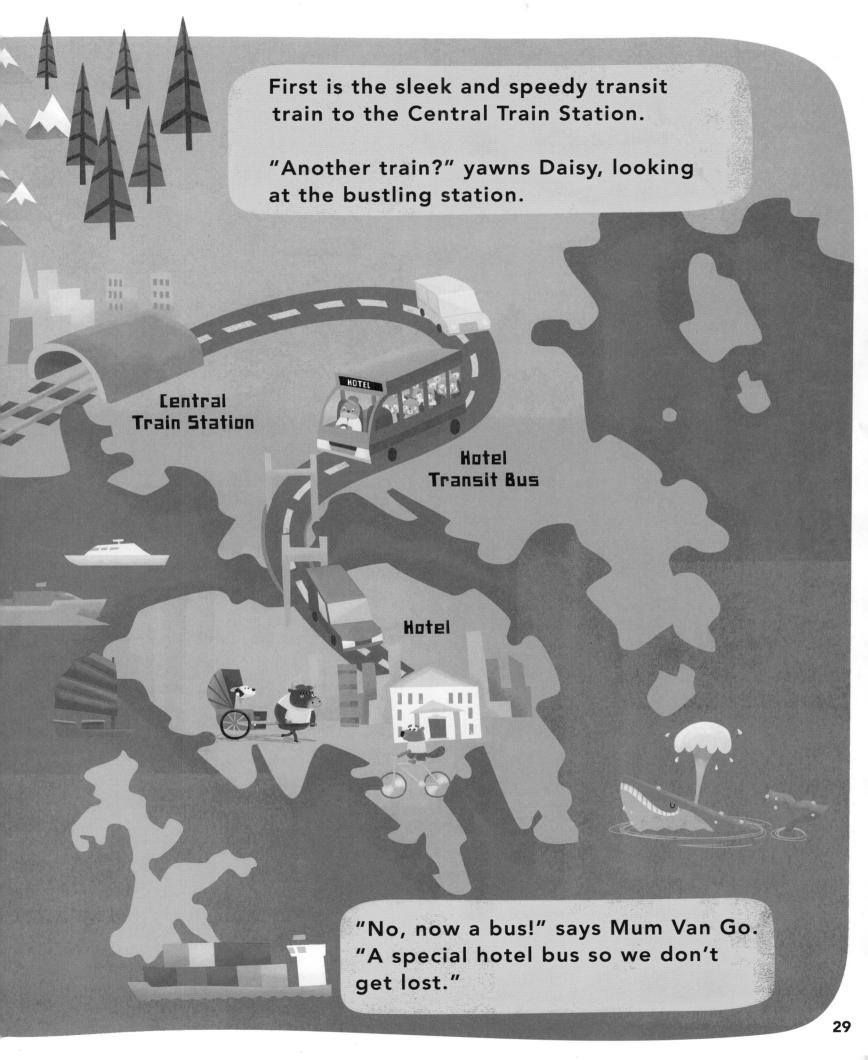

First is the sleek and speedy transit train to the Central Train Station.

"Another train?" yawns Daisy, looking at the bustling station.

Central Train Station

HOTEL

Hotel Transit Bus

Hotel

"No, now a bus!" says Mum Van Go. "A special hotel bus so we don't get lost."

In Hong Kong, they escape the bustle of the modern city and take the Star Ferry in Victoria Harbour.

"Look at all the boats!" shouts Freddie. The harbour is busy with tugboats, fishing boats and yachts zipping about.

"Fire! Fire!" They hear a shout from the harbour. Here comes the maritime fireboat to put out the flames as fire engines race along the shoreline. Soon the fire is out and everyone is safe.

They clap the brave firefighters.

Firefighters are brave all around the world.

* FIRE RESCUE *

FDNY - USA

Wild Fire Plane - AUSTRALIA

LFB - UNITED KINGDOM

SCDF - SINGAPORE, MALAYSIA

What a long flight from Hong Kong to their next stop – New York City, the Big Apple!

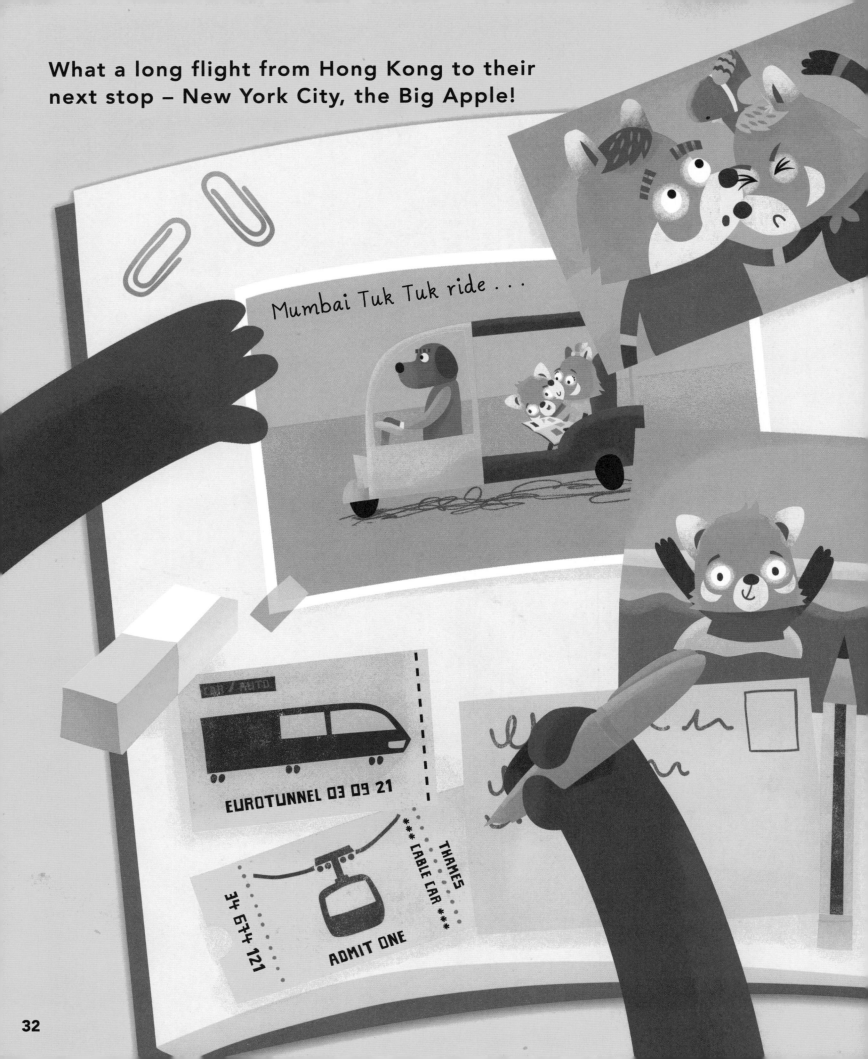

Mumbai Tuk Tuk ride . . . .

EUROTUNNEL 03 09 21

34 674 121

THAMES CABLE CAR ***

ADMIT ONE

Freddie and Daisy fill in a scrapbook diary of their travels so far.

They arrive early in New York, and they find everyone is wide awake and buzzing with activity!

"**Wow!**" says Freddie. "Look at all the yellow cars!"

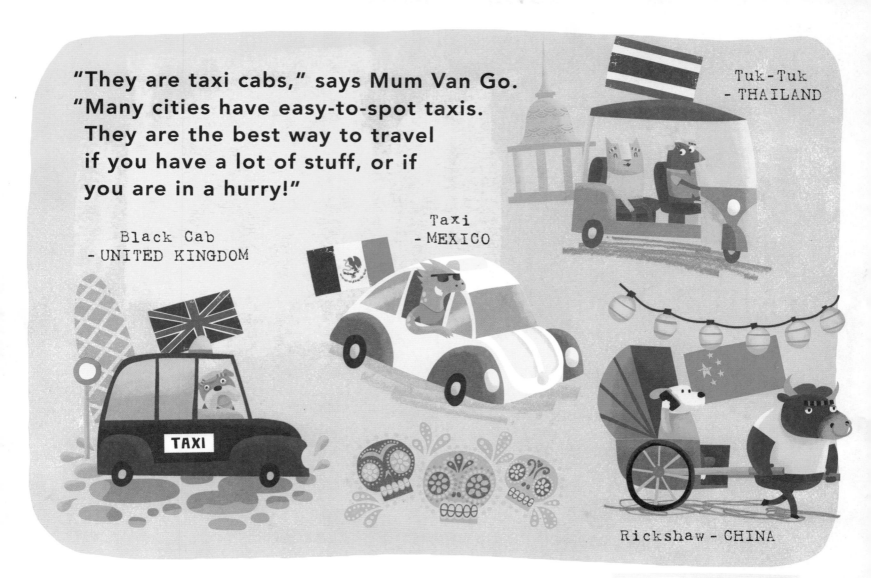

"They are taxi cabs," says Mum Van Go. "Many cities have easy-to-spot taxis. They are the best way to travel if you have a lot of stuff, or if you are in a hurry!"

Tuk-Tuk - THAILAND

Taxi - MEXICO

Black Cab - UNITED KINGDOM

TAXI

Rickshaw - CHINA

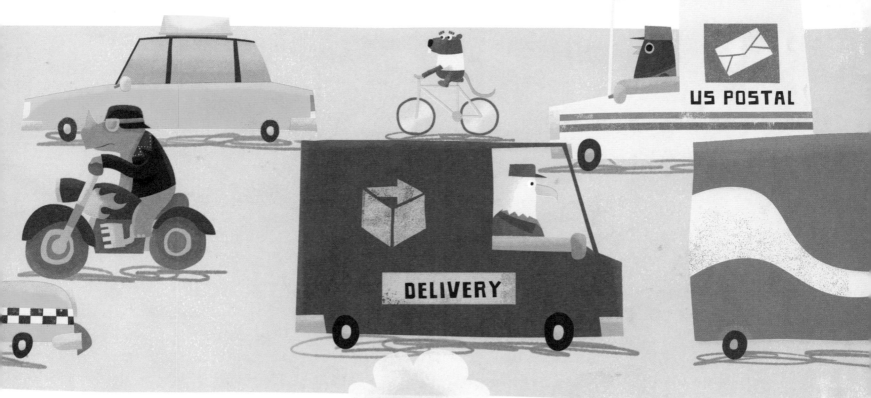

US POSTAL

DELIVERY

The family have an amazing time in New York but next stop is Peru. It's too far for a taxi, of course, so they head back to the airport.

In Peru, Daisy and Freddie are excited to go on an Amazon River cruise in a steam boat.

On the way, they spot river dolphins and monkeys.

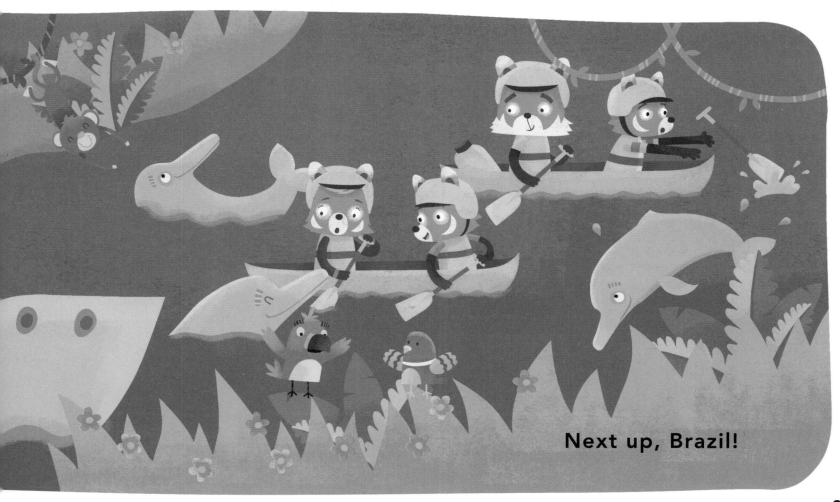

Next up, Brazil!

The Van Go family has planned a bike tour in Rio de Janeiro. They cycle with their tour guide looking at the water across beaches and lakes.

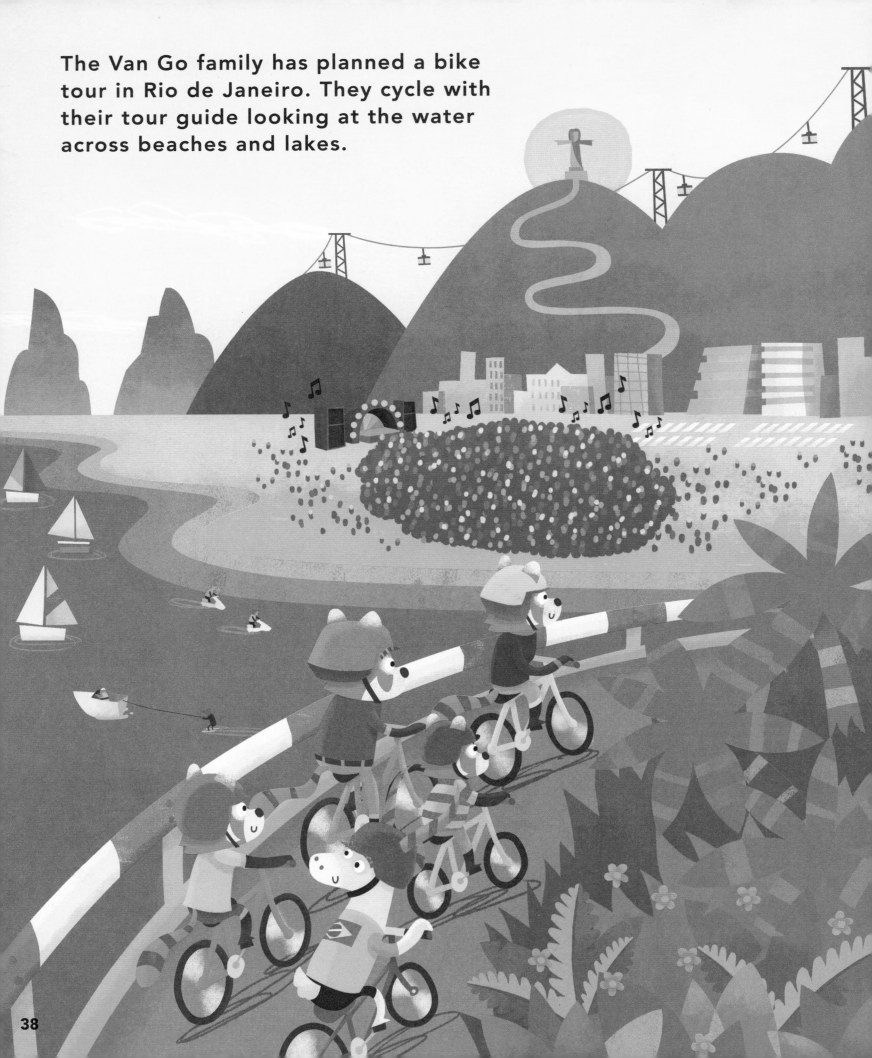

Whoops! Freddie takes a tumble and grazes his knee.
"I don't think you need an ambulance," smiles Dad, as he
dusts him down. "It's just a little graze. No bones broken."

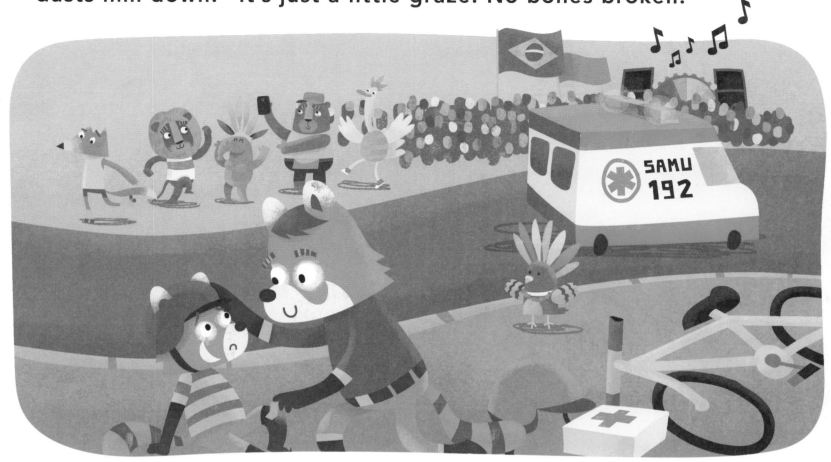

Freddie would quite like a ride in an ambulance in any city – he
thinks it would be thrilling to whizz along with the lights flashing.

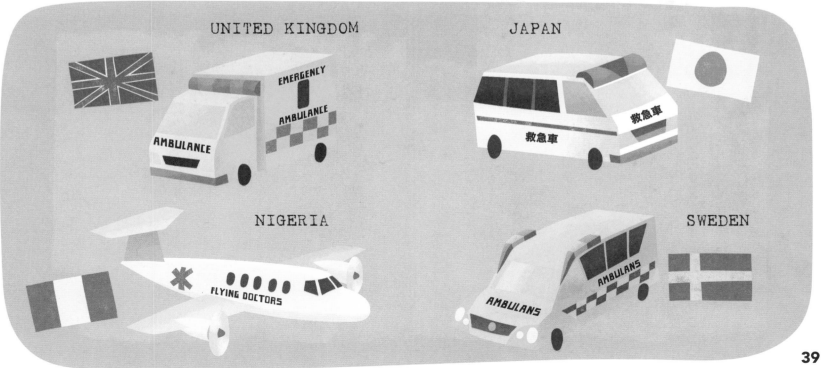

UNITED KINGDOM

JAPAN

NIGERIA

SWEDEN

BRAZIL

From Brazil to South Africa, it is a very long journey over the South Atlantic Ocean.

To pass the time, the Van Go family play a game: How long would it take to travel from Rio to Cape Town in different ways?

HOT AIR BALLOON
8 kmph = 752 hours

HELICOPTER
400 kmph = 15 hours

SUPERSONIC FIGHTER JET
2495 kmph = 2.5 hours

SPACE ROCKET
28,970 kmph = 12 mins

JUMBO JET
800 kmph = 7.5 hours

FINISH

SOUTH
AFRICA

In Cape Town, there is so much to see and do.

TABLE MOUNTAIN

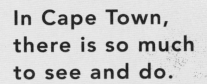

After breakfast in one of the friendly cafés on the Victoria and Alfred waterfront, they take the cable car to the very top of Table Mountain.

While Mum and Dad Van Go admire the view, Freddie looks down at the motorbike riders streaming along the mountain roads.

They are too far away to see the different types of bike but Freddie hopes his favourite – a chopper – is one of them.

Scooter - ITALY

Cruiser - JAPAN

Chopper - USA

Dirt track race bike
- GERMANY

The family are sad to leave Cape Town with its beautiful beaches and mountains. The next plane takes them 11,000 km from Cape Town to Brisbane, Australia.

"Our little blue van!" shout Daisy and Freddie, jumping for joy at the Camper Van Rental Company.

"One just like it," smiles Mum Van Go. "This fits us perfectly." They set off on the five-day Pacific Coast drive from Brisbane to Sydney.

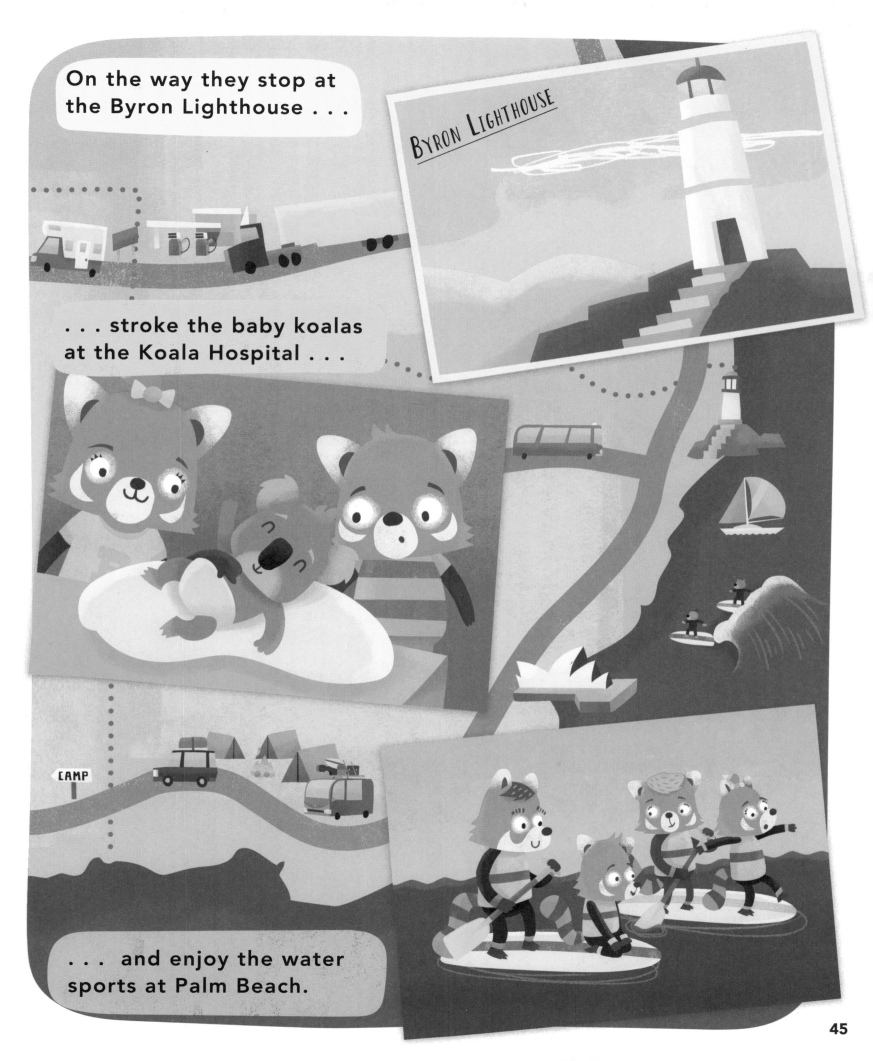

On the way they stop at the Byron Lighthouse . . .

BYRON LIGHTHOUSE

. . . stroke the baby koalas at the Koala Hospital . . .

CAMP

. . . and enjoy the water sports at Palm Beach.

45

Sydney Harbour is the busiest harbour they have ever seen.

The Van Go family look this way and that, from the famous Opera House facing out to sea to the huge ocean liners lit up like Christmas decorations along the harbour walls.

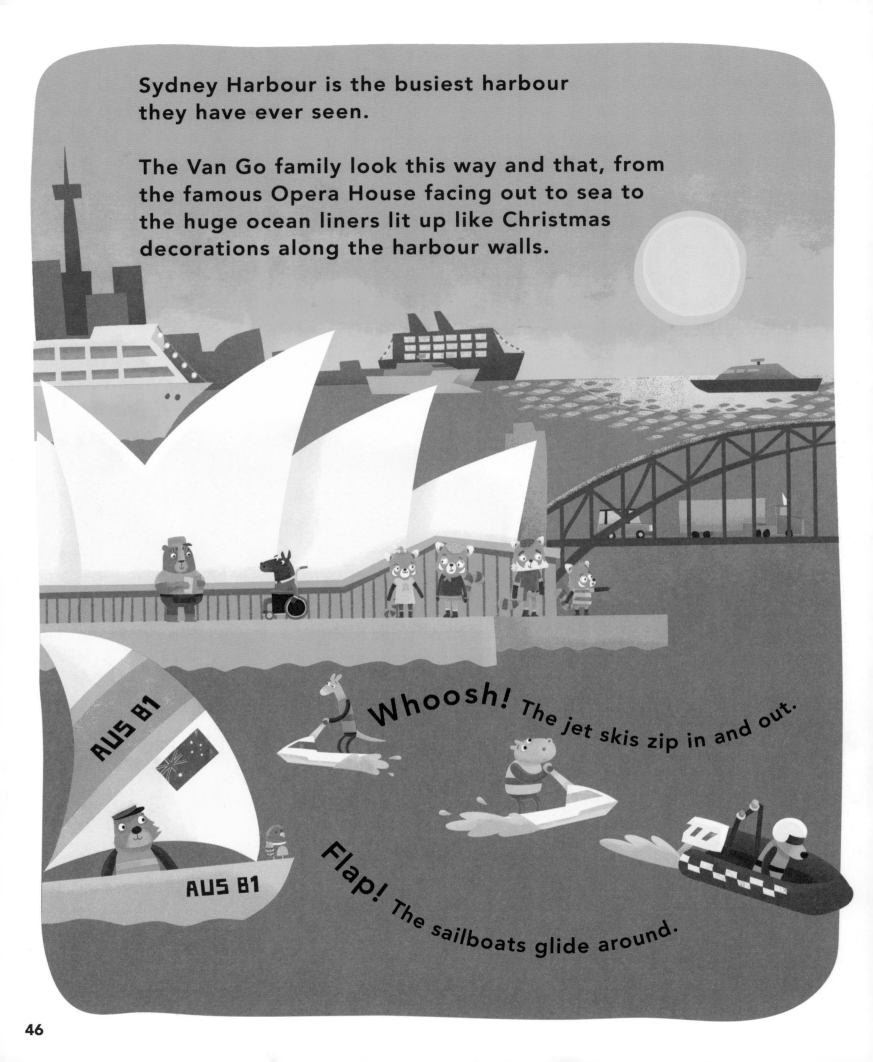

AUS 81

AUS 81

Whoosh! The jet skis zip in and out.

Flap! The sailboats glide around.

The last stop on the amazing world tour is New Zealand. As a special treat, they take a helicopter trip over Milford Sound and see penguins and seals basking in the sun.

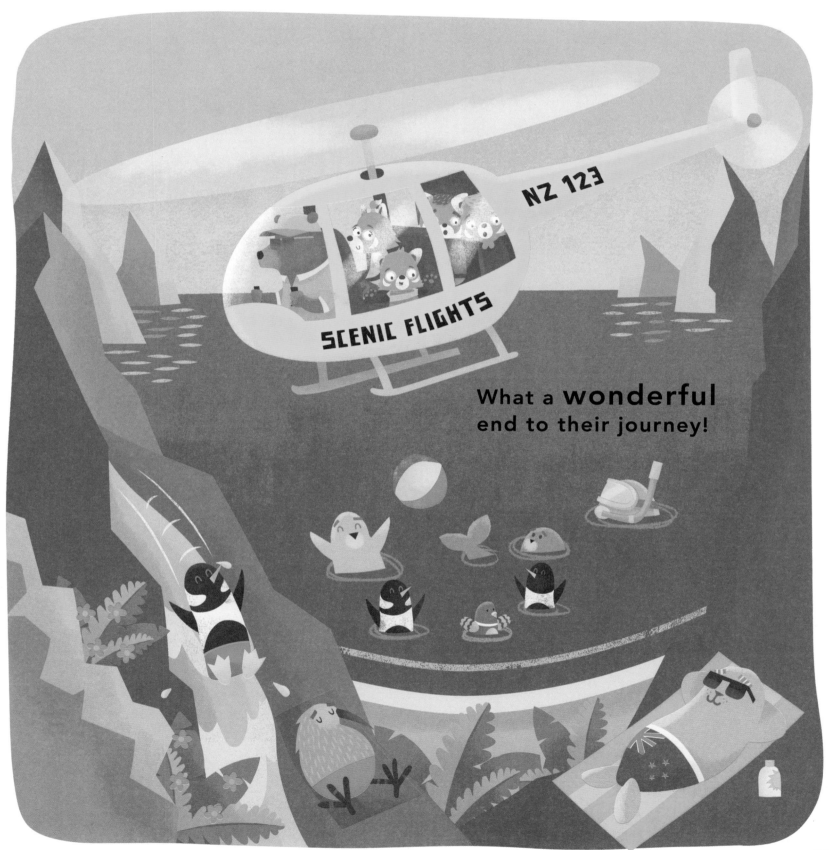

What a **wonderful** end to their journey!

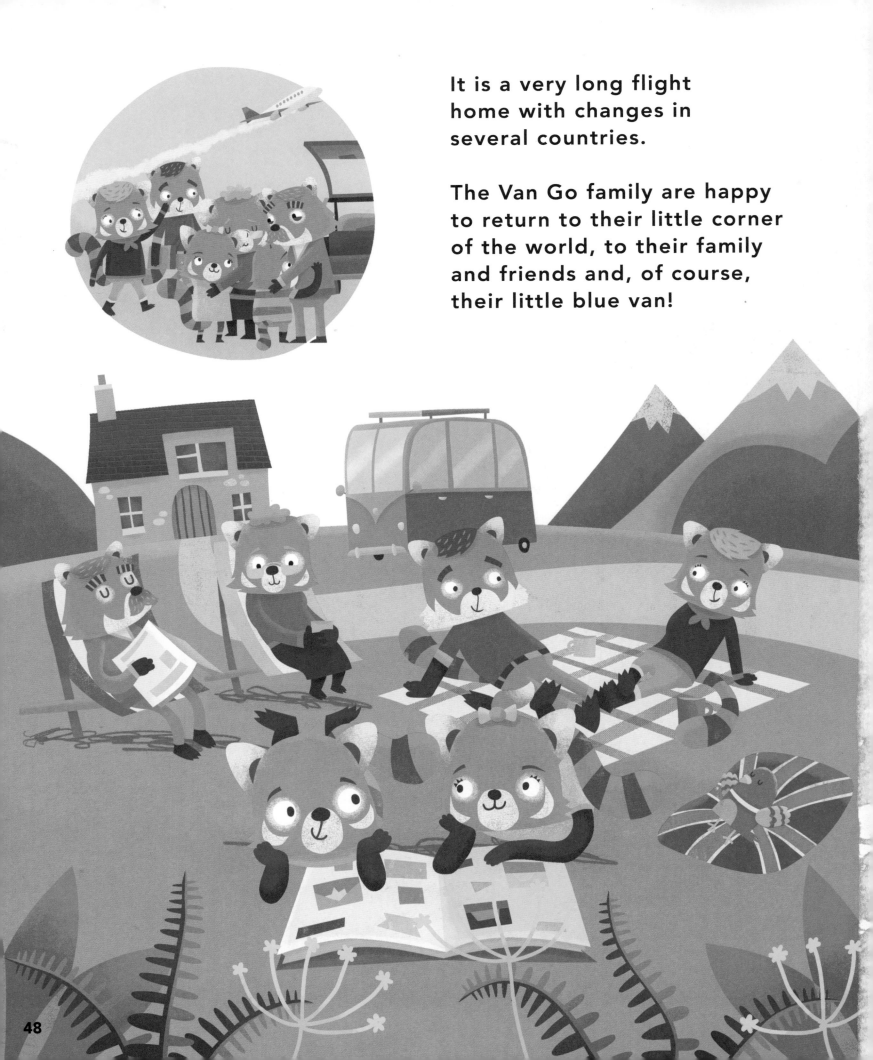

It is a very long flight home with changes in several countries.

The Van Go family are happy to return to their little corner of the world, to their family and friends and, of course, their little blue van!